DATE DUE

Demco, Inc. 38-293

THROUGH ARTISTS' EYES

Landscape and the Environment

Jane Bingham

Chicago, Illinois

Raintree

© 2006 Raintree
Published by Raintree
a division of Reed Elsevier Inc.
Chicago, Illinois

For information, address the publisher
Raintree, 100 N. LaSalle, Suite 1200
Chicago, IL 60602

Customer Service 888-363-4266
Visit our website at www.raintreelibrary.com

Editorial: Isabel Thomas, Patrick Catel, and Rosie Gordon
Design: Richard Parker and Tinstar Design www.tinstar.com
Picture Research: Hannah Taylor and Zoe Spilberg
Production: Duncan Gilbert
Originated by Chroma Graphics
Printed and bound in China, by South China Printing Company Ltd

10 09 08 07 06
10 9 8 7 6 5 4 3 2 1

Library of Congress Cataloging-in-Publication Data

Bingham, Jane.
Landscape and the environment / Jane Bingham.
  p. cm. -- (Through artists' eyes)
Includes bibliographical references and index.
ISBN 1-4109-2240-5 (library binding - hardcover)
1. Landscape in art-Juvenile literature. I. Title. II. Series: Bingham, Jane. Through artists' eyes.
N8213.B56 2006
712--dc22

2005024925

Acknowledgments

The publishers would like to thank the following for permission to reproduce photographs: **p. 21**, © 1990, Photo Scala, Florence/ Narodni Museum; **p. 32**, © 2005, Photo Scala, Florence/ Pushkin Museum; **p. 37**, © 2004, Photo Smithsonian American Art Museum/ Art Resource/ Scala, Florence; **p. 46**, © 2005, Digital Image, The Museum of Modern Art, New York/ Scala, Florence; **p. 51**, © 2005, Digital Image, The Museum of Modern Art, New York/ Scala, Florence; **p. 50**, © DACS 2006 Photo: © 1990. Photo Scala, Florence; **p. 33**, akg-images / JÉrÙme da Cunha; pp. 6, 7, Axel Poignant Archive; Bridgeman Art Library **pp.18-19** (© Ashmolean Museum, University of Oxford, UK), 16 (Fitzwilliam Museum, University of Cambridge, UK), 42 (© The Barnes Foundation, Merion, Pennsylvania, USA), 22 (© Tokyo Fuji Art Museum, Tokyo, Japan), 39, (© Yale Centre for British Art, Paul Mellon Collection, USA), 38 (Hamburger Kunsthalle, Hamburg, Germany), 40, (Musee Marmottan, Paris, France, Giraudon), 27, (National Gallery of Art, Washington DC, USA), 41, (National Gallery, London, UK), 20, (Prado, Madrid, Spain, Giraudon), 35, (Private Collection), 12 (Private Collection, Accademia Italiana, London), 14, 15 (Private Collection, Paul Freeman), 45, (Rushkin Museum, Moscow, Russia), 36, (Reynolds Museum, Winston Salem, North Carolina, USA), 5, (Rijksmuseum Vincent Van Gogh, Amsterdam, The Netherlands), 23, (Thyssen-Bornemisza Collection, Madrid, Spain, J.P.Zenobel), 13, (Victoria & Albert Museum, London, UK, The Stapleton Collection); Corbis **pp. 47** (Ansel Adams Publishing Rights Trust), 31, 49, (Bettmann), 26, (Buddy Mays), 25, (Hubert Stadler); **p.11**, Getty Images/ Photodisc; **p. 9**, South American Pictures/ Tony Morrison; **pp. 28, 29, 30**, www.britainonview.com.

Cover: *Evening at Milparinka NSW* (cibachrome colour photo) 1963 by Sir George Russell (1912-1981) reproduced with permission of Bridgeman Art Library/ National Gallery of Victoria, Melbourne, Australia, Gift of Lady Drysdale.

The publishers would like to thank Karen Hosack for her assistance in the preparation of this book.

The paper used to print this book comes from sustainable resources.

Contents

Any words that appear in bold, like this, are explained in the glossary.

Introduction

The sky is inky blue and is heavy with clouds. A violent wind rips through the field, making the corn ripple and sway. Crows swoop low, their jagged black shapes outlined against the sky. Straight ahead is a crooked path—but where does it lead, or does it simply come to an end?

This frightening scene is one of the last pictures painted by Vincent Van Gogh before he killed himself. The painting is much more than just a picture of a cornfield. It also reveals the artist's desperate state of mind.

Throughout his career, Van Gogh painted the countryside around him. Many of his paintings are filled with sunlight, but others show the land in a less cheerful mood. Van Gogh told his brother that he saw "sadness and loneliness" in the vast fields that surrounded him, but he also felt comforted by them. Even though his landscapes contain no people, they are filled with emotion. These powerful paintings clearly express the artist's feelings about himself and the world around him.

Artists and the landscape

Artists have responded to the land around them for thousands of years. Many have created pictures of the landscape. Meanwhile, other artists have chosen to make changes to the **environment**.

Some have created **land art** (large-scale **sculptures** in the land), while others have shaped their landscape into beautiful gardens.

In East Asia, the tradition of producing images of the natural landscape had been taking place since the 10th century C.E. In the West, landscape painting became fashionable in the 17th century. Before this, western painters tended to use landscape as the background of a portrait. However, after this late start, landscape painting developed in many interesting ways. Over the next few centuries, artists responded to their environment with a wide range of styles.

In addition to looking at painting, this book also covers land art and the art of garden making. Both these responses to the land have a very long history, and they are both still practiced today.

A range of art

This book ranges in time from 30,000 years ago to the present day. It also covers many countries of the world. To help you to see exactly where a work of art was made, there is a map of the world at the end of the book. The timeline on page 53 provides an overview of the different periods of history discussed in the book.

Town and country

Landscape paintings do not just show wild countryside. Some of the images discussed in this book show neat farmland or formal gardens, while others picture towns and cities. All these images are forms of landscape painting. They all present an artist's view of the world.

Looking at landscape

This book shows many different ways of looking at the landscape. It also asks a question: "What can these works tell us about the artists' feelings for the world around them?"

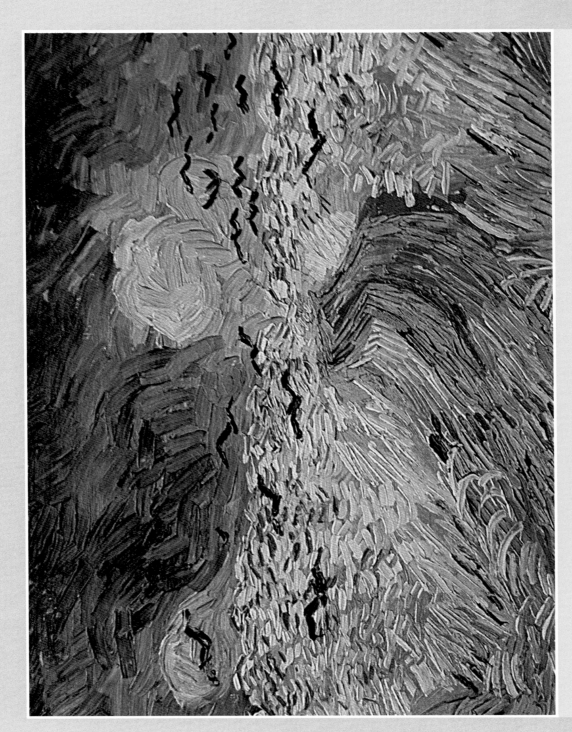

Vincent Van Gogh, *Landscape with Crows* (1890). In the last weeks of his life, Van Gogh concentrated on painting the landscape around him. The jagged brush strokes in this painting reflect the artist's tormented state of mind.

For over 40,000 years, the Aboriginal people of Australia have been making works of art about their land. Aboriginal art can take several different forms, including paintings, sculptures, and songs. All these works celebrate the powerful spirits that the Aboriginals believe created their land.

Legends of creation

Many Aboriginal works of art tell the story of the creation of the Australian landscape. According to Aboriginal beliefs, **Ancestor Spirits** journeyed through their land, creating all its features, such as rocks and streams. These journeys took place in a time known as the Dreamtime, and the routes that the Spirit Ancestors took are called the dreaming tracks.

Following the dreaming tracks

In traditional Aboriginal society, each new generation learns to retrace their Spirit Ancestors' steps. The **elders** of each tribal group, or **clan**, know the dreaming tracks for their area. At certain times of the year, the elders lead their clan through the landscape, following the path of the dreaming tracks.

In the course of their journey along the dreaming tracks, people sing songs and tell stories. This helps them to remember what happened at each stage of the Spirit Ancestor's journey. They also perform ceremonies associated with special events in the Dreamtime. In this way, the ancient dreaming tracks are never forgotten. Each Aboriginal clan keeps alive their part of the dreaming tracks through their art.

Uluru (Ayers Rock) in Australia is a **sacred** place for the Aboriginal people. It is featured in Aboriginal legends, songs, and paintings, and many ceremonies are performed around the rock.

An Aboriginal bark painting shows a legend from the Dreamtime, when the Spirit Ancestors created the land.

shimmering land

Many Aboriginal paintings include areas of crosshatched (crisscrossed) pattern. These patterns are made by painting a fine network of lines against a dark background. The areas of cross-hatched pattern are meant to look like desert land shimmering in the sun.

Sometimes they are shown as footprints. Stopping places are often indicated by a circle. There are also many other symbols with secret meanings. Only the artist, or a member of the artist's clan, can understand the full meaning of a painting.

Painting the dreaming tracks

For thousands of years, Aboriginal artists have been producing paintings that show the dreaming tracks. Traditionally, artists painted on panels of bark, using a range of natural **pigments** made from rocks and earth. However, since the 1970s, some artists have started painting on canvas, using man-made paints. By painting on large-scale canvases, artists can create enormous images of the dreaming tracks.

The paintings of the dreaming tracks work rather like a map. Sometimes the tracks are shown as wavy lines.

Changing the land

In many ancient cultures, people made dramatic changes to their environment. Some groups sculpted the earth into raised patterns. Some built circles from stones. Others made giant figures or other patterns on the ground. **Archaeologists** have many theories about the purpose of these ancient works of art, but nobody can be certain why they were created.

Mound sculptures

Around 3,000 years ago, some Native Americans in the northeast of the United States began to create raised "sculptures" in the landscape. They built a series of linked underground **tombs** for their chiefs. Then, they piled earth on top of the tombs, making raised patterns on the ground. Archaeologists believe that these mound sculptures have a religious purpose. Maybe the mounds were meant to be viewed from above by the gods?

The most famous surviving mound sculpture is the Great Serpent Mound in Ohio, which was created by the Adena people. This raised sculpture seems to show a serpent with an open mouth, and the serpent seems to be eating a circular object. Some experts think that the serpent is a god who is eating an egg. Others believe that the circular object shows the sun. They think that the mound represents the spirit of night consuming the daylight.

Medicine wheels

In the eastern Rocky Mountains, Native American people collected rocks and arranged them in patterns that look like giant wheels. These designs are known as medicine wheels.

More than 50 medicine wheels survive in the United States and Canada. Some appear to be 500 years old, while others may have been constructed 2,000 years ago. The medicine wheels probably marked sacred places, where people went to make contact with spirits. Some experts believe that the wheels were also used as basic calendars that recorded important sunrises and sunsets during the year.

Nazca lines

Around 2,000 years ago, the Nazca people of Peru, in South America, carved lines into the rocks of the desert. Some of these lines form giant geometric shapes. Others are images of animals and birds—including a monkey, a spider, and a hummingbird. The shapes made by the Nazca lines can only be recognized from the air. Experts disagree about the meanings of the Nazca lines. Some believe that the carvings were requests to animal gods to send rain. Other experts suggest that the ancient carved creatures pointed to places where people could find water.

This is a giant Nazca spider design seen from the air. The spider measures about 150 feet (45 meters) long and is formed by one continuous line.

Since the time of the earliest civilizations, people have created gardens. In this way, they shaped part of the land around them into a beautiful work of art. Different civilizations have created very different styles of garden.

Gardens in the desert

The earliest known gardens were created in the deserts of the Middle East. Around the 9th century B.C.E., some rulers became rich enough to build themselves palaces. The palaces were surrounded by gardens, where the rulers and their families could relax. We know about these gardens through the work of early painters, carvers, and writers.

Assyria and Babylon

Around the year 879 B.C.E., King Assurnasipal II of Assyria (present-day Syria) gave orders for a magnificent palace to be built. Some ancient Assyrian carvings survive showing the king and queen in their palace gardens. Even though the palace was built in a dry, desert area, the carvings show tall palm trees, trailing vines, and ponds filled with lotus flowers. Inside their paradise garden, the Assyrian king and queen relaxed on couches while musicians sang to them.

Another famous garden in the desert was built by King Nebuchadrezzar II of Babylon (in present-day Iraq). Nebuchadrezzar's wife was homesick for the green hills of her homeland, so the king created an amazing garden for her inside the city walls. The hanging gardens of Babylon were planted on a series of terraces. Water was constantly pumped up to the top of the gardens and tumbled down the sides of the terraces in waterfalls.

Islamic water gardens

Ever since the time of the city of Babylon, the Persian people have created beautiful water gardens featuring pools and fountains. This tradition has spread throughout the **Islamic** world.

One of the most famous Islamic gardens was built by the **Moors** in Grenada, in southern Spain. The 14th-century gardens at the Alhambra in Grenada are made up of a series of shady courtyards. Each courtyard is planted with flowers and has its own fountain or decorative pool. Later, the **Mughals** in northern India created elaborate water gardens for their palaces. The series of water tanks in the gardens of the Taj Mahal act like a set of mirrors, reflecting the perfect architecture of the Taj.

The Taj Mahal and its formal water gardens were completed in 1653. The gardens surrounding the Taj are an essential part of the building's total design.

Roman gardens

The Romans created elegant gardens with flowerbeds, ponds, statues, and fountains. They also painted garden scenes on the walls of their villas. One **fresco** from a townhouse in Pompeii shows a delicate marble fountain standing in front of a bed of trees, bushes, and flowers.

Some Roman gardens were incredibly grand. The gardens surrounding Emperor Hadrian's villa at Tivoli were carefully landscaped with ponds, waterfalls, and fountains. Hadrian's garden also contained several buildings in Roman, Greek, and Egyptian styles.

Medieval gardens

During the **Middle Ages**, people created formal gardens for growing herbs and flowers. These gardens had many small flowerbeds, which were separated by low hedges or paths. At the center of the garden there was often a fountain or a well.

Medieval gardens were usually surrounded by walls. Within the grounds of a castle, the walled garden was a private place. Here, the lady of the manor and her **ladies-in-waiting** could gather flowers and play music and relax together. In abbeys and monasteries, the peaceful herb garden formed the center of a courtyard, called a cloister.

This detail is from a fresco found in the Roman city of Pompeii. The Romans often covered the walls of their villas with charming garden scenes.

This Mughal miniature painting shows a prince and princess relaxing in the formal gardens of their palace.

Paintings of gardens

Many paintings of gardens have survived from the Middle Ages. Sometimes artists showed real gardens, but they also painted imaginary ones.

In some medieval paintings and poems, the garden is a secret place where lovers can meet. In the love poem "The Romance of the Rose," the lover declares his love for his lady inside a rose garden. This was a favorite subject for artists.

Some medieval artists showed heaven as a flower garden. Inside the heavenly garden, angels took care of the plants and trees or sat on carpets of flowers playing music. Each flower in the paradise garden had a special meaning. For example, lilies represented purity.

Mughal miniatures

Between the 16th and the 18th centuries, Mughal artists in northern India painted delicate miniature paintings. Many Mughal miniatures showed young women relaxing in beautiful gardens. One popular garden scene was painted again and again. It showed a young girl singing as she rode on a garden swing.

Landscapes and Gardens of the East

Landscape painting began in China in the 10th century C.E., during the rule of the Song emperors. Chinese artists created dramatic scenes with towering boulders, misty valleys, lakes, and waterfalls.

Changing styles

In the early Song period, artists painted detailed **watercolor** scenes, using mainly greens and blues. Later painters developed a freer and simpler style, using just black ink. They dipped their brushes in the ink and made rapid brush strokes on the paper. By the end of the Song period, in the 13th century C.E., many Chinese artists were combining watercolors and ink.

One of the greatest early landscape artists was Guo Xi, who lived in the 11th century. He was the first Chinese painter to move from painting wide views to concentrating on a few interesting details. Guo Xi often painted rocks surrounded by swirling water, with a few plants or trees clinging to their surface.

Guo Xi developed the technique of making the foreground of his pictures stand out clearly while the background was shrouded in mist. He believed in the importance of understanding nature in all its moods. He said that in order to paint a landscape, the artist had to visit the scene at all times of day and in all types of weather.

The ancient traditions of landscape painting are still practiced in China today. Artists still create dramatic images in watercolor and ink showing rocks, trees, water, and gently swirling mists.

This Chinese river scene was painted in the 18th century. While some Chinese landscape artists showed wild countryside, others created scenes filled with buildings and people.

Willow pattern plates

In the 18th century, Chinese artists painted garden scenes on china plates and bowls. These designs were copied by the English china manufacturer Thomas Minton. Minton's blue-and-white "willow pattern" china became very popular in the West. It is still manufactured today.

Chinese gardens

The Chinese tradition of creating formal gardens began over 1,000 years ago. The early Chinese emperors sculpted the landscape to create tiny mountains and islands. This miniature landscape was meant to show the heavenly land where the Chinese gods lived.

Traditional Chinese gardens feature rocks, ponds, and willow trees. They also include gates, bridges, and occasional temples. These gardens are places where people can be calm and quiet. Visitors can walk or sit quietly in these gardens and enjoy the beauty of nature.

Gardens often feature in designs for Chinese porcelain. This 18th-century plate was produced for export to Europe. It shows a lady and her maid walking by a lake.

Japanese landscape prints

During the 18th century, a distinctive style of printmaking developed in Japan. Japanese prints are simple but bold. They combine strong lines with large blocks of color. At first, Japanese printmakers concentrated on images of people, but by the 1800s they had become very interested in landscape. The two great Japanese masters of landscape were Hokusai and Hiroshige. They both worked in the early 19th century.

Katsushika Hokusai, *South Wind, Clear Dawn*. This is from the series *36 Views of Mount Fuji*, created between 1830 and 1835. In these prints, Hokusai uses a limited range of colors to create his striking designs.

Hokusai and Hiroshige

Hokusai was fascinated with every aspect of nature. He studied the same landscapes at all times of day and created hundreds of images of waterfalls, waves, trees, and mountains. Hokusai's most famous landscapes are his 36 *Views of Mount Fuji*. These striking images show the blood-red mountain, streaked with snow and standing out starkly against a deep-blue sky. Mount Fuji is a sacred mountain for the Japanese, and many Japanese people try to make a **pilgrimage** to its summit (top). Hokusai's prints are more than just an image of a famous landmark. They are also studies of a very holy place.

For most of his working life, Hiroshige concentrated on landscapes. His best-known series of prints is 69 *Stopping Points on the Coastal Road from Edo to Kyoto*. Hiroshige achieved extraordinary effects with color, gradually fading from intense tones to the merest hint of color.

Japanese gardens

During the 5th century C.E., the Chinese introduced the idea of gardens to Japan.

Like the Chinese garden, the Japanese garden is a peaceful place where people can think about the beauties of nature. Japanese garden designers show great respect for nature but also include some man-made elements. The usual elements of a Japanese garden are water, garden plants, stones, waterfalls, trees, and bridges.

There are several different types of Japanese garden. The "tea garden" contains a special arrangement of buildings leading to a teahouse, where people can take part in the tea-drinking ceremony. The "strolling garden" is the largest type of Japanese garden. It presents the walker with many changing views.

The Japanese "sand and stone garden" is extremely simple. It is created from raked white sand, with five groupings of fifteen stones arranged in clusters of two, three, and five. Sand and stone gardens are often found in **Buddhist** monasteries. They are intended to help people **meditate** and reach a state of happiness and peace.

Japanese influences

By the 1860s, Japanese prints had reached Paris. They created a wave of enthusiasm for Japanese art that lasted for the next 40 years. The Japanese style of landscape painting had a powerful impact on the work of the French **Impressionists**, especially Monet and Cézanne (see page 40).

Landscapes of the Renaissance

During the 15th century, some artists in Italy were inspired by the ancient artwork of the Greek and Roman empires. They were impressed by the way these artists had studied nature so accurately in their work. The period from 1400 C.E. onward, when artists tried to learn from and improve on this **classical** art, is known as the **Renaissance**. This means "rebirth." For 200 years, the new style of painting and sculpture spread throughout Europe.

Italian landscapes

The artists of the Italian Renaissance often painted scenes from Greek and Roman legends. These scenes often took place in an imaginary landscape.

The landscape featured ruined classical buildings, woods, streams, hills, and distant mountains. It was based on the real countryside of Italy.

The birth of perspective

The artists of the Italian Renaissance tried to create landscapes with depth. They struggled with the problem of how to show things in the distance.

Around the year 1400, some artists realized that things looked smaller as they got farther away. They figured out a system for showing things in the distance. The system is known as **perspective**.

Perspective involves drawing a series of lines to a point in the painting where all the lines meet. Artists use perspective lines as a guide to help them create scenes with depth.

Uccello's forest

One of the first artists to experiment with perspective was Paolo Uccello, who worked at the start of the 15th century. His painting *The Hunt in the Forest* shows a group of mounted hunters chasing after deer who disappear into the depths of the forest. In this intriguing painting, Uccello has followed the rules of perspective very carefully, making his trees smaller and smaller as they get farther away.

A distant haze

In the late 15th century, some artists noticed that distant landscape features had a hazy, almost smoky appearance. They created a new technique to show this effect in paintings. The technique is known as *sfumato*, which comes from the Italian word for smoke. The sfumato effect is achieved by gradually blending one color into another, so that there are no sharp outlines. Leonardo da Vinci used the sfumato technique in the background of his famous portrait, the *Mona Lisa*.

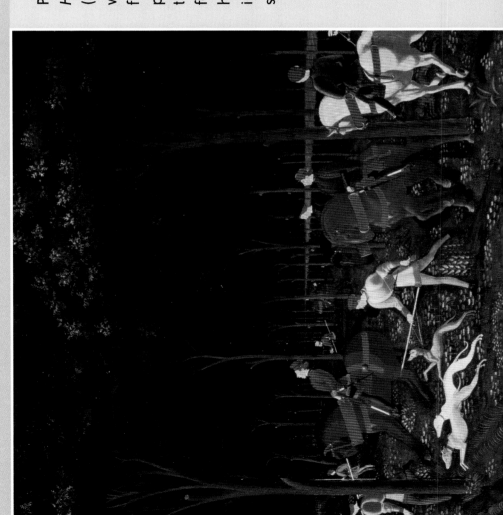

Paolo Uccello, *The Hunt in the Forest* (c. 1470). Uccello was one of the first artists to use perspective. In this picture of a forest at night, he has succeeded in creating a real sense of depth.

A northern view

The Renaissance took place in northern Europe as well as Italy. By the mid-15th century, artists in the Netherlands, England, and Germany were painting in a much more **realistic style than before.**

Most of the northern artists concentrated on painting portraits and religious scenes. However, some of their paintings included stunning views of the wild northern countryside, as glimpsed through windows and arches. Two outstanding artists who included views of the landscape in their work are Albrecht Dürer and Pieter Bruegel.

Dürer's landscapes

The German artist Albrecht Dürer was a great painter and printmaker who also made incredibly detailed drawings from nature. Dürer's drawings include realistic images of animals and plants. He also produced careful studies of the countryside. Later, Dürer used these landscapes as backgrounds in his paintings.

In the fall of 1494, Dürer traveled to Italy, where he remained until the following spring. During this trip, he painted a number of bold watercolor paintings of the Alps. Dürer's alpine landscapes are painted in broad strokes, with some areas roughly sketched in detail. He uses mainly dark colors, which give a sense of mystery and depth.

Dürer used his landscape studies when he painted his first self-portrait in 1498. Here, he shows himself as a young man sitting at a window, while beyond the window is a stunning view of alpine scenery.

Albrecht Dürer, *Self-Portrait with Gloves* (1498). This portrait of the artist as a young man offers an intriguing glimpse of the Italian Alps. The painting reveals Dürer's fascination with landscape.

Bruegel's scenes

The painter Pieter Bruegel lived in Antwerp, in present-day Belgium. He painted scenes of town and country life filled with lively figures. Bruegel created a series of detailed paintings showing his local landscape in different seasons. Today, five of these paintings still survive.

The Corn Harvest shows a cheerful summer scene, with golden fields of corn beneath a blue sky. The houses nestle snugly in the valleys and, in the distance, a misty sea can be glimpsed. The winter scene, *Hunters in the Snow*, has a very different feeling. In this painting, the sky is almost black.

The dark trunks and branches of the trees form a stark contrast with the snow-covered ground. The houses and fields in the valley are blanketed in snow, while ice-capped mountains rise in jagged peaks behind them.

Town and country

Many of Bruegel's paintings concentrate on towns. During the 16th century, many people moved from the country to work in cities and towns. Bruegel's scenes of town life reflect this new kind of urban society.

Pieter Bruegel the Elder, *Haymaking* (1565). The painting shows country people gathering in the harvest. While the foreground is filled with activity, the background is a study of the Belgian landscape, with its towering rocks and distant mountains.

The Birth of Landscape Painting

True landscape painting began in the Netherlands in the 16th century. Joachim de Patinir, who died in 1524, was the first person to describe himself as a landscape painter. Patinir's paintings usually show religious subjects. However, his figures are often very small, so that the landscape is the first thing you notice. The figures in Patinir's paintings were often painted by other artists while the master concentrated on the landscape.

Most of Patinir's paintings show a very wide view, known as a **panorama**. His dramatic landscapes have a mysterious, storybook feel. They are filled with exciting details such as castles perched on rocky crags, bridges over rushing streams, or calm expanses of deep-blue water.

Early landscape artists

Patinir was soon followed by other northern artists who specialized in landscape paintings. The German painter Albrecht Altdorfer also painted religious scenes set in enormous landscapes. Altdorfer based his landscapes on the wooded and mountainous countryside around the Danube River, but he made their scenery more **melodramatic**. The 16th-century Dutch painter Gillis van Coninxloo was also influenced by the German countryside. He spent much of his working life in Germany, creating striking scenes framed by tall trees.

Two Dutch masters

During the 17th century, many talented landscape artists worked in the Netherlands, but the two most outstanding figures were Jacob van Ruisdael and Rembrandt van Rijn.

Jacob van Ruisdael lived from 1628 to 1682. He has been called Holland's greatest landscape painter. Ruisdael began his career painting the flat countryside and river **estuaries** of the Dutch coast. These early paintings show peaceful scenes beneath vast, cloudy skies.

Albrecht Aldorfer, *Mountain Range* (c. 1530). Altdorfer loved the wildness of the German countryside. His early landscapes were filled with witches, wild men, and other weird creatures.

Later, however, Ruisdael traveled inland to more wooded and varied countryside. Ruisdael's later landscapes show waterfalls, pine forests, and hills under stormy skies.

The great Dutch master Rembrandt van Rijn produced many different kinds of landscapes, including wild, imaginary scenes, views of towns and rivers, and wide panoramas. But he returned most often to simple country scenes.

Rembrandt produced dozens of studies of Dutch farms and cottages sheltered by trees, in a landscape of flat fields.

Most of Rembrandt's landscape studies were black ink drawings. Using just pen and ink, Rembrandt explored the shapes made by buildings and trees. He enjoyed showing the different textures of the ancient cottage walls and their thatched roofs. He also experimented with the effects of light and shade, painting dramatic, inky shadows.

Jacob van Ruisdael, *Winter Landscape* (1670). Ruisdael was a master at creating atmosphere. Here, he creates the feeling of a bleak northern landscape, threatened by brooding storm clouds.

Classical Landscapes

In the 17th century, many painters in Italy and France tried to create the perfect classical landscape. This was not a real place, but an artistic idea of how the countryside of ancient Greece and Rome once looked.

The classical landscape featured wooded hills, lakes, streams, and the ruins of ancient temples. Two outstanding painters in this style were the Italian artist Salvator Rosa and the French artist Nicolas Poussin. However, the great master of the classical landscape was Claude Lorrain.

Claude Lorrain

Claude Lorrain lived from 1604 to 1682. He was born and raised in France, but he spent a large part of his career working in Rome, surrounded by ancient Roman ruins. He often created an imaginary classical landscape, scattered with ruined temples.

Claude usually painted scenes from classical legends, but the most important element of his pictures was their landscape setting. Claude was fascinated by the "mood" and atmosphere of a landscape, and this was the real subject of his paintings. Sometimes Claude produced oil paintings in rich colors, but often he used **sepia** tones—a range of different shades of brown. His dramatic landscapes are full of contrasts between light and dark. They also have a very convincing sense of depth, with a foreground, a middle ground, and a distant background.

Claude was famous for producing very well-balanced pictures. He planned his landscapes very carefully so that no single feature stood out too much. Claude's paintings presented the ideal "picturesque" landscape. Many later artists copied the style of his landscapes.

Italian gardens

Painters were not the only ones who tried to recreate the classical landscape. In the 15th century, some wealthy Italian landowners began to pay designers to create elaborate gardens for their houses. These gardens contained carefully planted bushes and trees, but also incorporated Roman statues and the ruins of Roman buildings.

One of the most famous early Italian gardens belongs to the Villa D'Este in Tivoli. The garden was created in the 16th century and included the remains of ruined buildings from the nearby villa of the Roman emperor Hadrian. Many artists sketched the gardens. Then, they used elements from the Tivoli gardens in their paintings of classical scenes.

The Gardens of the Villa D'Este in Tivoli were created on a steep hillside close to the ruins of Hadrian's villa. With their magnificent fountains and statues, they provided an inspiration for artists.

French and English Styles

During the 17th century, a grand style of garden design became fashionable in France. Wealthy **aristocrats** paid garden designers to create a series of raised garden terraces that dropped down gradually from the house. Each terrace had its own formal flowerbeds, ponds, and fountains, and the terraces were linked by wide gravel avenues and flights of stone steps. At the top and bottom of the flights of steps were impressive stone statues. The whole garden was designed to impress the viewer with a sense of magnificence and order.

The gardens of Versailles

The most famous grand French garden was created for King Louis XIV at Versailles. In addition to a series of terraces, these gardens have many large ponds and fountains. The gardens at Versailles were built at a time when the French royal family was at its most powerful. The grand stretches of trees and water somehow give the impression that the king has managed to take control of nature.

This view is from the terrace of the Palace of Versailles. King Louis XIV's magnificent gardens include huge ponds, decorative fountains, avenues of trees, and miniature forests known as groves.

Rococo style

Watteau and Fragonard both painted in the **Rococo** style. This style first developed in France and was popular in Europe throughout the 18th century. Rococo scenes were painted in a soft, dream-like way. They included details such as delicate flowers, interlacing ribbons, and scrolls. Some people laughed at this style of painting because they saw it as too light and unimportant. Others loved it because the pictures were full of feelings about love and harmony.

Jean-Honoré Fragonard, *The Swing* (c. 1765). Fragonard's characters are posed in a beautiful landscape. All of Fragonard's landscapes are slightly unreal, like very attractive stage sets.

Outdoor fun and games

In the 18th century, some artists in France began to paint scenes of elegant young men and women in the countryside. These paintings had nothing to do with the hard-working lives of the poor French peasants. Instead, the painters portrayed carefree young aristocrats having fun in a beautiful country setting.

The two main artists of this style of outdoor painting were Jean-Antoine Watteau and Jean-Honoré Fragonard. Some of Watteau's paintings show young people picnicking or dancing together, while others show young men singing love songs to their ladies. The peaceful landscape backgrounds to these playful scenes feature elegant, spreading trees and distant fields.

Several of Fragonard's most famous paintings feature a richly dressed young woman seated on a swing hanging from the branches of a tall tree. This woman and her companions are all extremely unsuitably dressed for the countryside, as if they are just playing at country life.

Developments in England

During the reign of the **Tudors** and **Stuarts**, the English developed some interesting garden designs. They concentrated on creating formal gardens on a smaller scale than the gardens in Italy and France.

Meanwhile, English artists painted views of country houses and their gardens. The main aim of these paintings was to show the landowner's lands, rather than the English countryside.

Patterned gardens

Most English gardens of the Tudor period were divided into many smaller areas, rather like a patchwork quilt. These small gardens-within-a-garden were planted with low hedges and plants.

Often, the hedges and plants were grown in interwoven patterns known as knot gardens. Sometimes hedges were planted in the shape of a **maze**. Raised grass walkways known as mounts ran all around the garden. The mounts allowed people walking in the garden to view the patterns from above.

Knot gardens

Sometimes the spaces in between the knot garden hedges were filled with herbs or flowers, but often hedges of contrasting colors made up the whole design. These different-colored hedges crossed over each other, just like ribbons, to form a complicated knot. The patterns in an Elizabethan knot garden were often based on patterns in embroidery or **tapestry**.

This formal flower garden is at Hampton Court Palace, in England. The Hampton Court gardens were laid out in the 16th century. They include some fine examples of topiary, which is the art of clipping hedges into interesting shapes.

Mazes

Maze patterns made from low hedges were planted in English gardens from the Tudor period onward, but the most famous English maze was constructed in 1690 at the royal palace of Hampton Court. Unlike the earlier mazes, Hampton Court maze has tall hedges, so it is possible to become completely lost inside it. Mazes like this are known as baffle mazes. In the 17th century, it became fashionable in Europe for the owners of grand houses to include a baffle maze on their grounds.

Making mazes

People have been creating mazes in the landscape since the time of the ancient Egyptians. In medieval Europe, people created mazes from turf and carved maze patterns on rocks. The Hopi people of North America also created mazes. They believed that by following the path of a maze, it was possible to reach a greater understanding of nature and the forces of creation. Today, people still design mazes. Some are permanent structures made from stone or hedges. Others are temporary, constructed from straw and other materials.

The maze at Hever Castle in Kent, England, was created in the early 20th century, but it is based on a maze design found in Tudor gardens.

Ideas from Italy

By the 18th century, "classical" landscape paintings by artists such as Claude Lorrain (see page 24) had become very popular in England. Some rich young landowners decided to travel to Italy to see for themselves the landscapes that had inspired Claude's painting. While they were in Italy, they viewed the Roman ruins and made sketches of the landscape. They also bought drawings and paintings by Claude and other artists.

A new style of garden

When the rich young Englishmen returned from their travels, they were determined to create classical landscapes in Great Britain. They paid talented designers to create a new style of garden.

The two leading garden designers in 18th-century England were Humphry Repton and Capability Brown. Humphry Repton worked on over 200 gardens. He invented the term *landscape gardening*. Capability Brown designed many English gardens. He created landscapes that appeared to be completely natural, with hills and lakes and clumps of trees. He also included charming classical buildings and statues as part of his total landscapes.

Capability Brown designed Stowe Landscape Gardens, in England, in the 1740s. The gardens include a large lake, several temples, and a grotto.

This is the Governor's Garden in colonial Williamsburg. In the United States, early gardens usually had formal flowerbeds. In the 18th century, Thomas Jefferson led a movement toward less formal gardens.

The Claude glass

Some visitors to Italy tried to see the landscape through the eyes of the painter Claude Lorrain. In order to help them achieve this aim, they looked at the countryside through a "Claude glass." This was a glass panel that was tinted brown. It allowed them to see the landscape in the brownish sepia tones that Claude often used in his paintings.

Jefferson's garden

The new style of "natural" gardening introduced in England soon spread to the United States. In 1786 Thomas Jefferson, who was later to become the president of the United States, toured the gardens of England, including Blenheim Palace, which was designed by Brown. Jefferson was very impressed by the English landscaped gardens and planned to create a similar garden for his home, Monticello, in Virginia.

Jefferson's garden plans included a waterfall and a grotto as well as buildings in the Greek and Chinese styles. He also planned to fill his garden with tame deer, peacocks, hares, and pheasants. In the end, most of these plans were abandoned, but the Monticello Garden still features a "natural" landscape, including clumps of trees carefully planted to look like English woodland.

Romantic Landscapes

Around the end of the 18th century, some people began to see the countryside in a new way. They stopped wanting to tame nature and began to appreciate the wild and romantic character of their landscape. These artists and writers were part of the **Romantic** movement.

The Romantic movement

Romantic artists, writers, and musicians believed in the importance of feelings and emotions. They were excited by the beauty and power of the natural world and tried to show nature in all its "moods."

Many Romantic artists and writers also found inspiration in the mysterious world of legend and fairy tale. The Romantic movement was especially popular in Germany and Great Britain.

Caspar David Friedrich

One of the greatest Romantic painters was the German artist Caspar David Friedrich. Friedrich lived in east central Germany, close to the mountains. He studied the countryside around him at all times of day.

Friedrich's landscapes often show mountain scenes, moonlit seas, and morning mists. His paintings convey a strong sense of the different moods of nature and of the power and mystery of the natural world. In particular, the light in his paintings seems to be mysterious and unearthly.

A fairy tale landscape

During the 19th century, many people in Germany became very interested in their country's legends and fairy tales.

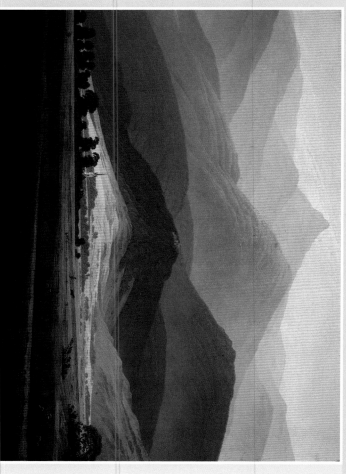

Caspar David Friedrich, *Riesengebirge Landscape* (1810). Friedrich was fascinated by the changing effects of light. In this painting, he has perfectly captured the effect of sunlight on the meadows.

Romantic painters created images of fairy tale castles perched on top of mountains. Poets retold the ancient legends, and the **composer** Richard Wagner wrote a series of operas in which a knight searches for a magic ring through a land of mountains, rivers, and castles.

Some wealthy landowners helped to create a real romantic landscape in Germany. They built fairy tale castles along the banks of the Rhine River. The most dramatic of all these castles was Neuschwanstein, which was built by King Ludwig of Bavaria.

The king's white, mountain-top home, with its cluster of turrets, looks just like a castle in a Romantic painting.

Beethoven and the landscape

The great composer Ludwig van Beethoven was a leading member of the Romantic movement. He was inspired by the rocky scenery and rushing rivers of Germany and also by the softer elements of the German landscape. Beethoven named his sixth symphony "The Pastoral" (which means "about the countryside") because it expressed some of his feelings about the German landscape.

Although it looks like a medieval castle, Neuschwanstein Castle was built in the late 19th century. It was the home of King Ludwig II of Bavaria. Ludwig's aim was to create a fairy tale castle based on the romantic legend of the swan knight.

John Constable

The English painter John Constable found beauty in the everyday details of the English countryside. Constable said that his art could be found "under every hedge." He was fascinated by the effects of light and shade in the landscape and created hundreds of oil painting sketches at different times of the day, in all weather.

Constable developed a new technique for capturing the constant movement of light in nature. He used a **palette knife** to add flicks of white paint. When Constable exhibited these paintings, the public disliked them, naming his technique "Constable snow."

Even though many people today think Constable's work shows relaxed, realistic images of English country life, the paintings are actually very carefully constructed. Constable was influenced by the methods of 17th-century Dutch landscape painters. He experimented with their ideas and his oil painting sketches in his studio.

J. M. W. Turner

The outstanding Romantic landscape painter in England was Joseph Mallord William Turner. Turner lived from 1775 to 1851. In the early years of his long career, he tried out different styles of landscape painting, first copying the Dutch realist artists and then producing paintings in the style of Claude (see pages 24–25). He also constantly sketched from nature.

In his oil and watercolor studies, Turner experimented with using bold colors and making his brush strokes very free and loose. By the 1830s, Turner had developed a style of his own. In his stunning paintings of sunsets or storms at sea, realistic landscape details became much less important than atmosphere. Turner's paintings are almost Impressionist in style (see page 40). They give a feeling of nature's power and energy.

William Wordsworth

Artists were not the only ones to respond to the wild, romantic side of nature. The English Romantic poet William Wordsworth grew up surrounded by mountains and lakes, where he learned to love and fear the power of nature. His poems describe the beauty, violence, and splendor of the natural world.

Light and movement

John Constable aimed throughout his life to show the constant movement and sparkle of the countryside. He said he tried to capture "the dews—breezes—bloom and freshness, not one of which has yet been perfected on the canvas of any painter in the world."

John Constable, *Dedham from Langham* (c. 1815). Constable went to school in the English village of Dedham, and he painted the countryside around Dedham hundreds of times. Some of Constable's paintings are filled with detail, but in this picture he uses a loose, almost sketchy style.

The Hudson River School

During the 19th century, landscape painting really took off in North America. Thomas Cole is often known as the father of American landscape. He was influenced by Constable's English landscapes. However, he adapted his style to show the wild countryside around his home in the Catskill Mountains.

Cole founded a group of landscape artists known as the Hudson River School. These painters all aimed to show the spirit of the untamed landscape of the United States. They concentrated on painting the countryside north of New York, in the valley of the Hudson River, with the rugged Catskill Mountains in the distance.

Bierstadt and Church

Two outstanding members of the Hudson River School were Albert Bierstadt and Frederic Edwin Church. At the start of his career, Bierstadt worked alongside some of the earliest landscape photographers in the United States. Like his photographer friends, the young painter aimed to show wide panoramas. Bierstadt painted scenes around the Hudson River, but also made several painting trips to the Midwest. His work is strongly Romantic in style. He often painted sunsets and mists, and his pictures have a powerful atmosphere.

Thomas Cole, *Home in the Woods* (1847). The members of the Hudson River School did not just paint what they saw. They aimed to create a romantic image of their new nation. This painting presents an idealized view of the lives of the American settlers.

Frederic Edwin Church was a student of Thomas Cole's who loved to spend time hiking and sketching in the countryside. Church traveled to South America and to Alaska and produced famous paintings of rainforests and icebergs. He was also famous for his dramatic studies of Niagara Falls. Church's works are very dramatic, with rising mists and highly colored skies.

Back to nature

By the 1800s, many Americans were living in towns and cities. This worried some people, who thought that the American people were becoming cut off from the natural world. These people formed a "back-to-nature" movement.

They moved out of the cities and tried to live a simple life in the country. The romantic paintings of Hudson River School encouraged people to join the back-to-nature movement.

The main figure in the back-to nature movement was the thinker and writer Henry Thoreau. In 1845 Thoreau went to live on his own in the woods of Massachusetts. He built a wood cabin by a pond and lived mainly on beans that he grew himself. Thoreau lived in the woods for two years and kept a journal of his daily experiences. Later he published a book called *Walden, a Life in the Woods*. *Walden* immediately became an American classic.

Albert Bierstadt, *Among the Sierra Nevada Mountains, California* (1868). This romantic scene was the result of a painting trip to the American West. Bierstadt was stunned by the astonishing scenery of the Sierra Nevada mountain range.

The Barbizon School

In the mid-19th century, a new group of landscape artists formed in France. The group was based in the village of Barbizon, close to the forest of Fontainebleau, which is south of Paris. The group rejected the style of classical painters such as Claude and Poussin. Instead, they aimed to paint fresh, realistic scenes of French country life.

The Barbizon painters showed real landscapes and people and often painted their pictures in the open air. This was a dramatic new move, since artists had previously made sketches outdoors and painted the finished pictures in their studios.

The leading member of the Barbizon group was Théodore Rousseau. He specialized in woodland scenes, painting clusters of tall trees and clearings in the forest. Rousseau was very interested in the changing effects of light and painted the same scene at many different times of day.

Rousseau's friend, Jean-François Millet, came from a poor country family and hated towns and cities. His paintings of the countryside often included peasants hard at work in the fields. Millet used a limited range of colors and a loose brushwork style to create his images of a flat farming landscape.

The third major figure in the Barbizon school was Charles-François Daubigny.

During his lifetime, Daubigny was often criticized for his rough, sketchy style. However, he created some stunning river scenes, viewed from his boathouse studio. The work of the Barbizon artists was not completely understood at the time, but they had a powerful influence on the French Impressionists (see page 40).

Théodore Rousseau, *In the Wood at Fontainebleau* (c. 1850). Rousseau concentrated on the effects of light and shade, rather than painting in every detail. This was rather like the French Impressionist painters.

Visionary landscapes

Some artists in the 19th century took inspiration from real landscapes and transformed these into paintings of landscapes from their imaginations. The English artists William Blake, John Martin, and Samuel Palmer all produced astonishing imaginary landscapes inspired by personal religious visions.

The English poet and painter William Blake wrote poetry about an imaginary kingdom called Albion. He illustrated his poems with striking watercolor paintings. Blake's kingdom of Albion was an ideal vision of his homeland, without the ugly factories and towns that were part of 19th-century Britain. His paintings of Albion show a magical land with inky, jagged mountains under scarlet skies.

Another English artist, John Martin, painted scenes from the Bible set in a landscape of boiling skies, crumbling cities, and towering mountains. Martin's visionary scenes were popular with the public, and his exhibitions attracted far larger crowds than Turner's.

Palmer's paradise

The 19th-century artist Samuel Palmer combined his observations of the real world with a personal vision of paradise. He produced detailed paintings and ink studies of the Vale of Shoreham in southern England. These magical landscapes show a "valley of vision" where contented workers lived a carefree life and trees were weighed down with golden fruit. Many of Palmer's landscapes are lit by the ghostly light of a massive moon.

This sketch of the Vale of Shoreham, by Samuel Palmer, emphasizes the magical character of the artist's "valley of vision."

New Ways of Seeing

Around the end of the 19th century, a group of French painters continued to develop the techniques of capturing movement and light that were started by Constable and Turner. Instead of making sketches outside and completing work in a studio, the Impressionists tried to finish their paintings in one sitting. This quick way of working gave their paintings a feeling of freedom.

The Impressionists were helped by the introduction of ready-mixed tubes of oil paint with screw-on caps. This made painting outside easy. Before then, artists had to mix their own paint in the studio and throw it away as it dried up.

The Impressionist movement spread fast, and soon painters all over Europe and in North America were painting in this new and exciting style.

Claude Monet

One of the founders of the Impressionist movement was the French artist Claude Monet. Monet saw many different colors in the landscape—especially as the light changed during the day. For example, when he looked at a hay field, he realized that he did not only see straw colors. He saw purples and greens, pinks, and yellows in the parts that reflected the sun.

Monet explored his impressions of color in many exciting, experimental paintings. In his works, the many colors that make up the total "impression" are painted in hundreds of feathery strokes that each blend gently into each other. In addition to painting hundreds of landscapes, Monet created a famous series of paintings showing haystacks at different times of day.

Claude Monet, *Impression, Sunrise* (1872). Monet was one of the leaders of the Impressionist movement. When the Impressionists first started to show their work, many people were shocked by the artists' bold brush strokes, vivid colors, and lack of attention to detail.

Monet's waterlilies

Monet kept on experimenting throughout his long life. In his final years, he concentrated on painting his garden at Giverny, in France. Monet painted a series of enormous paintings of his waterlily pond, in which the petals, leaves, and water created almost **abstract** patterns.

Pointillism

Some Impressionist artists conducted some fascinating experiments with color. They realized that all colors are made by mixing together the three **primary colors:** red, yellow, and blue. But instead of mixing these colors to create their paints, they allowed the viewer's eyes to do the mixing.

Pointillist artists painted thousands of tiny dots—or "points"—onto their canvases, in different colors.

When a pointillist painting is viewed from a distance, all the dots combine to form different shades. The result is a lighter and brighter impression of color than can be created by mixing paints. Two leading pointillist artists were Georges Seurat and Camille Pissarro. They created landscapes that seem to sparkle with light, although they are strangely lacking in depth. However, pointillist painting was very time-consuming, and the pointillist movement never really took off.

Georges Seurat, *Bathers at Asnières* (1884). Seurat used his pointillist technique to create an impression of sparkling light in the landscape. This technique was especially effective for showing water.

Paul Cézanne, *Red Earth* (c. 1890–1895). Cézanne built up his pictures from geometric shapes and blocks of color.

Paul Cézanne

Paul Cézanne was strongly influenced by the Impressionist movement, but he developed a very personal style. He did not paint directly from nature, but sketched many details and put them together later to form a carefully composed total scene.

Cézanne's landscapes are often framed by tall trees. Within this frame, each element in the scene is carefully arranged to create an impression of balance and harmony. The shapes made by features of the landscape often take the form of squares, rectangles, and triangles. This use of basic, geometric shapes influenced the **Cubist** movement (see panel). Cézanne also used color in a very individual way. He applied each color in short strokes to form a detailed pattern of patches throughout his painting.

Cézanne was influenced by the work of the Japanese printmakers (see page 16). He admired the Japanese artists' sense of composition and their confident use of color and line. Cézanne studied Hokusai's series of views of Mount Fuji and painted many views of his local mountain, Mount Saint Victoire.

Cubism and the landscape

Cézanne said, "Nature should be handled with the cylinder, sphere, and cone."

However, in his paintings, these basic geometric shapes are softened by his use of color. Other 20th-century artists followed the rules of Cubism more strictly. Pablo Picasso and Georges Braques both produced Cubist studies of the landscape. These scenes were painted in neutral colors, and all the landscape features were shown as bare geometric shapes.

Cubism

The Cubist movement began in the early years of the 20th century with the ideas and work of Georges Braque and Pablo Picasso. Cubist painters built up their pictures using a collection of geometric shapes. They created a complex image by showing an object or a scene from several different points of view. Cubism lasted until the 1920s and helped to pave the way for the development of purely abstract art.

Brilliant colors

Around 1905, a new group of painters emerged in France. They used vibrant colors and rapid, broken brush strokes to create scenes that seemed to be filled with sunshine. The leading artists of this group were Henri Matisse, André Derain, and Maurice de Vlaminck. When they exhibited their striking landscapes, they were nicknamed the Fauves, which means "wild beasts."

Painters at Pont Aven

In the 1880s and 1890s, a group of artists in northwestern France developed their own approach to landscape. These artists were based around the village of Pont-Aven, on the coast of Brittany. They had deliberately moved away from the cities and settled in this remote part of France so that they could be part of a peaceful, rural way of life. The leader of the group was Paul Gauguin.

The Pont Aven artists painted bold, simplified landscapes using large areas of flat, vivid color. Many of their landscapes show the rocky coast of Brittany and include striking figures dressed in traditional costumes. In their bold but simple compositions, the French artists were strongly influenced by Japanese landscape prints.

A very personal view

One of the most individual landscape painters of the 19th century was Vincent Van Gogh. He used vibrant colors and rapid, swirling brush strokes to create a landscape that seems to be almost alive (see page 5).

In his later years, Van Gogh suffered from serious mental illness. He experienced periods of intense **depression and anguish**, and many of his later landscapes reflect his troubled state of mind. These disturbing scenes often feature enormous suns, gnarled and hollow trees, and pierced and twisted rocks.

Van Gogh's later landscapes are filled with a terrifying energy. Simply by looking at these paintings, you can sense the power of the sun beating down on the dried-out land. You can also feel the strength of the wind bending the trees in its path and rippling through the corn. In these disturbing landscapes, Van Gogh manages to convey the message that nature can be both cruel and frightening.

Gauguin in Tahiti

When he was 43, Gauguin moved to the island of Tahiti, in search of a natural way of life that was not affected by the modern world. He was strongly influenced by the art of the South Pacific, with its simple forms and vivid colors, and his paintings became much simpler and bolder than before. Gauguin's images of the Tahitian landscape are made up of clearly outlined blocks of color that create a patterned, almost patchwork effect. These later paintings show the powerful impact that the tropical landscape had on his senses and emotions.

44

Paul Gauguin, *Landscape with Peacocks* (1892). In this striking painting, Gauguin uses vivid colors and swirling shapes to show the exotic, tropical landscape of the island of Tahiti.

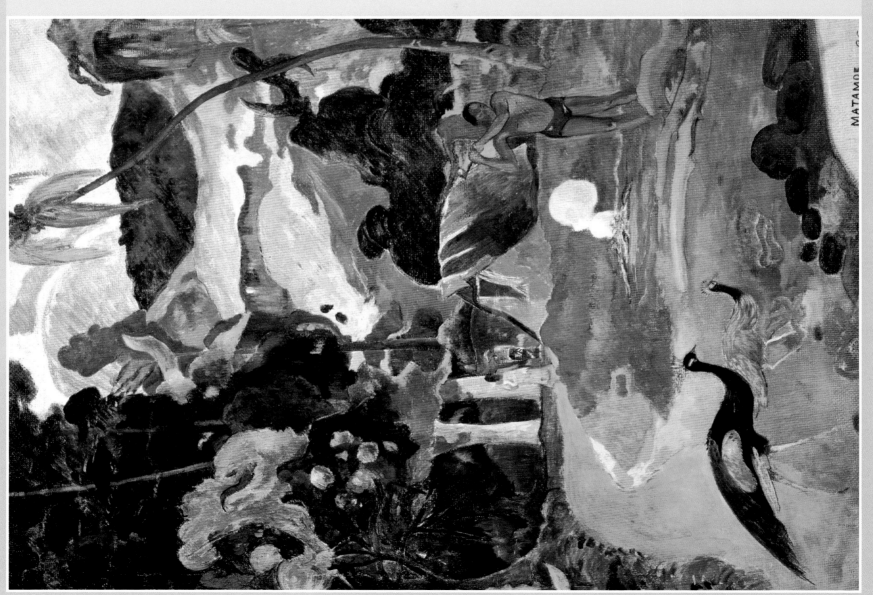

Images of the United States

During the 20th century, some artists produced distinctive images of the United States. These pictures did more than just show the landscape. They also gave an impression of how it felt to live in the United States. Edward Hopper conveyed the sense of a vast and lonely country through his paintings of deserted gas stations and empty roads stretching out into flat, open countryside. He also painted haunting images of the coast, with houses and lighthouses perched on the very edge of the land.

Andrew Wyeth's landscapes with lonely figures have a similar sense of the smallness of human life in the vast American landscape.

Wyeth's most famous painting, *Christina's World*, shows a young girl in the middle of an enormous wheat field, with two dark farmhouses standing menacingly at the top of a hill. The image gives a sense of the frightening possibilities of life in a landscape that can be unfriendly.

A very different image of the United States is given by Richard Estes. He paints views of city streets, with towering skyscrapers and **billboards**. Estes's style is very realistic but, like the Hopper landscapes, his scenes are almost deserted. The U.S. cities that he paints are largely fantastic creations of dream cities, sparkling and gleaming in the sun. He seems to be showing us a vision of how the United States might be.

Andrew Wyeth, *Christina's World* (1948). This painting of a young girl's world suggests a vastness and emptiness in the American landscape.

Ansel Adams, *Aspens, Northern New Mexico* (1958). Adams was fascinated by the wildness of the American landscape. Many of his photographs convey a sense of the mystery of the United States' unexplored wilderness areas.

Photographing the United States

The American landscape has also been portrayed by some outstanding photographers. In the early 20th century, Ansel Adams traveled all over the western states with his camera. His dramatic black-and-white photos give a powerful impression of the size and grandeur of the American wilderness. Another early North American master of photography, Alfred Stieglitz, concentrated on cityscapes. Some of Stieglitz's most memorable images show ghostly city streets covered in a shining blanket of snow.

Australian landscapes

Since the 1950s, some Australian painters have produced powerful images of their land. Fred Williams conveys the **elemental** power of the **Australian outback** in his almost abstract images of a harsh, red land, scattered with strangely shaped rocks. Sidney Nolan shows the adventures of the Australian folk hero Ned Kelly, set against a cruel landscape of boulders, scrub, and sand.

New Visions of the Land

In the 1960s, artists in Europe and North America began to be interested in a new kind of sculpture known as land art. Land art usually involves changing the landscape, either by adding objects to it or by rearranging the land with earth-moving equipment.

Although land art has been recently rediscovered, it is in fact an ancient art form. People have been creating art within their landscape for thousands of years (see pages 8–9).

Altering the landscape

Some contemporary artists change the landscape by creating mounds, ditches, and mazes. These structures are often inspired by ancient earthworks. One of the best-known examples of a piece of land art that altered the environment is Robert Smithson's *Spiral Jetty*. This impressive sculpture was built in the basin of the Great Salt Lake, Utah, and forms a giant spiral pattern made from rocks and salt crystals. Smithson says that this work is strongly influenced by the mysterious spiral mounds created by the Adena people (see page 8).

Adding to the landscape

Sometimes artists add objects to a landscape to change it in some way.

The Bulgarian artist Christo uses fabric to transform the landscape, wrapping trees or buildings in brightly colored cloth. One of Christo's largest projects was *Running Fence*, a curtain-fence that snaked its way over more than 24 miles of Californian countryside. With its billowing folds of cloth, Christo's "fence" highlighted the natural shapes of the landscape.

Other artists place objects in the landscape, such as giant concrete tunnels, structures shaped like temples, and even half-buried cars. All of these works of art are intended to make the viewer see both the landscape and the objects in a new way.

Understanding the land

Some land art records the artist's experience of a landscape. The British artist Richard Long has turned the act of walking through the countryside into a kind of art. Long uses photographs, maps, and notes to provide a record of his walks, which he displays in a gallery **installation**. He also collects materials from his journey, such as rocks, and assembles them into sculptures in the gallery. By visiting a Richard Long exhibition, people can share the experience of walking through the landscape.

Giant art

Some land art covers vast areas. Michael Heizer's *Nine Nevada Depressions* consists of nine curved and zigzagging trenches dug into the surface of the Nevada desert. The trenches look like giant, abstract doodles and extend over a total span of 520 miles.

Christo, *Pont Neuf*, Paris (1986). Christo has created several land art projects using fabric. Here, a bridge in Paris is wrapped in orange cloth. What effect does Christo's work have on this urban landscape?

Abstract landscapes

Some artists have used landscape as a starting point for exploring abstract patterns and forms. Two outstanding painters who moved from painting landscapes to creating abstract images are the Swiss painter Paul Klee and the Russian painter Wassily Kandinsky.

Paul Klee visited Tunisia, in North Africa, in 1914. There, he was delighted by the clear shapes, huge skies, and brilliant colors of the desert. Klee painted a series of desert landscapes that became increasingly simple and abstract. These landscapes explored geometric shapes, using a combination of squares, triangles, and rectangles for the buildings and a vast, circular disc for the sun. In these paintings, Klee also experimented with brilliant stripes of color, as the tones of the sky gradually merged into the desert horizon.

In Klee's later works, he mainly concentrates on simple geometric shapes. However, the influence of the early landscape paintings can still be seen in his patterns of brightly colored triangles and squares and his horizontal color stripes.

Paul Klee, *Little Pine Tree* (1922). In many of his pictures, Klee represents the landscape with simple shapes. This painting suggests a pine tree growing on a rocky hill.

Wassily Kandinsky's paintings are completely different from Paul Klee's. In these colorful compositions, Kandinsky assembles a crowded collection of symbols and shapes. Some of the shapes are purely abstract, but others are based on the Russian landscape, showing jagged mountains, rolling hills, and rainbows.

Patterns and shapes from nature

The patterns and shapes of the landscape have provided an inspiration for many abstract artists. The British painter Bridget Riley uses her art to recreate the visual effects of nature. Through a series of colored lines and shapes, she tries to reproduce the same effects that viewers experience when they see light shining through leaves or sparkling on waves.

The sculptors Henry Moore and Isamu Noguchi both created abstract sculptures whose gentle curves are deliberate reflections of forms in the landscape.

What next?

At the start of the 21st century, artists all over the world are still creating images of their landscape. Some are trying to show exactly what they see. Others are using the landscape as a starting point for different forms of art. People are also responding to their environment by creating gardens and making land art. At a time when many people are worried that our environment is under threat, the land all around us is still a very important subject for artists.

Bridget Riley, *Fission* (1963). Riley has explained that her paintings are inspired by shapes seen in nature. This painting explores the kind of shapes formed by rolling hills or waves.

Map and Further Reading

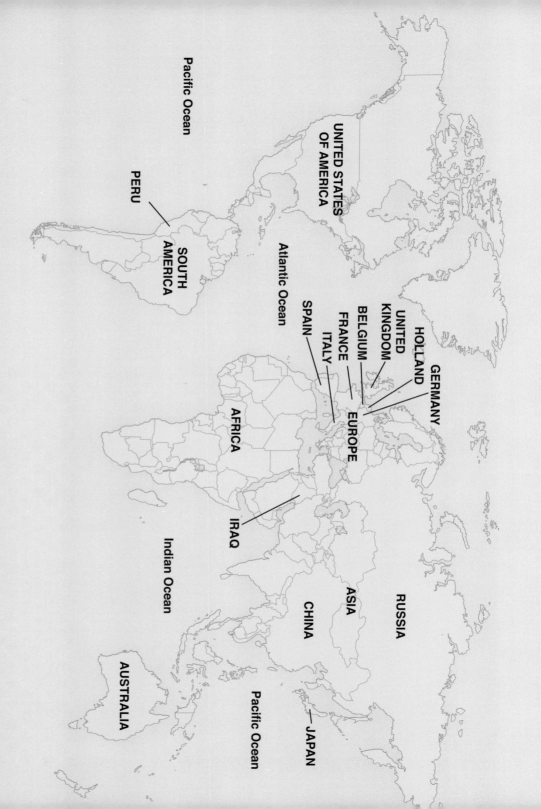

Pacific Ocean

UNITED STATES
OF AMERICA

PERU

SOUTH
AMERICA

Atlantic Ocean

SPAIN

ITALY
FRANCE
BELGIUM
UNITED
KINGDOM
HOLLAND

GERMANY

EUROPE

AFRICA

IRAQ

RUSSIA

ASIA

CHINA

JAPAN

Indian Ocean

Pacific Ocean

AUSTRALIA

Map of the World

This map shows you roughly where in the world some key works of art were produced. The countries marked on the map relate to entries in the Timeline, opposite.

Further Reading

Heinemann Library. *Art in History* series. Chicago: Heinemann Library, 2006.

Heinemann Library. *Artists in Profile* series. Chicago: Heinemann Library, 2003.

Heslewood, Juliet. *The History of Western Painting: A Young Person's Guide.* Austin, Tex.: Raintree Steck-Vaughn, 1995.

Raintree. *World Art and Culture* series. Chicago: Raintree, 2006.

Welton, Jude. *Eyewitness Art: Looking at Paintings.* New York: DK, 1994.

Timeline

This timeline provides dates for some key works of art. Many of these dates are approximate, and are simply intended to give a rough idea of when the works were produced. The entries are linked to countries marked on the Map of the World, opposite.

B.C.E.

c. 30,000 Aboriginal people in Australia begin to create images of their land. This tradition has continued until the present day.

c. 800 Assyrian artists show beautiful palace gardens (modern-day Iraq)

100s Roman artists paint frescoes featuring elegant gardens

The Nazca people of Peru carve large-scale designs on rocks

C.E.

c. 900 Landscape painting begins in China

c. 1100 The Adena people of Ohio build the Great Serpent Mound (U.S.)

1100s Artists in Europe start to paint images of gardens

1490s Albrecht Dürer makes studies of the landscape (Germany)

c.1500 Joachim de Patinir is the first artist to describe himself as a landscape painter (Belgium)

1560s Pieter Bruegel the Elder paints a series of landscapes with figures (Holland)

1630s Claude Lorrain starts to paint the Italian landscape

1640s Jacob van Ruisdael begins to paint the Dutch landscape

Rembrandt van Rijn starts his studies of Dutch farms and cottages

1740s Capability Brown starts to design landscapes for English country homes

1790s J. M. W. Turner starts to create his landscapes (UK)

c.1810 Casper David Friedrich starts to paint romantic images of the German countryside

1820s John Constable begins to paint the English countryside

c.1830 Hokusai begins to produce his *36 Views of Mount Fuji* (Japan)

1830s Thomas Cole founds the Hudson River School of landscape painters in the United States

1840s Theodore Rousseau founds the Barbizon School of landscape painters in France

1870s Claude Monet start to paint the French countryside in an Impressionist style

1890 Dutch artist Vincent Van Gogh paints *Wheatfield with Crows*

Paul Cézanne begins to create landscape paintings influenced by Cubism (France)

1930s Ansel Adams starts to photograph the American landscape

1950s Bridget Riley begins to create her landscapes (UK)

1970 Robert Smithson creates *Spiral Jetty* (U.S.)

1976 Bulgarian artist Christo creates *Running Fence* in California (U.S.)

Glossary

Aboriginal people people who have lived in a country for thousands of years, before later settlers arrived

abstract showing an idea rather than a thing

ancestor family member who lived a long time ago

anguish misery and suffering

archaeologist someone who studies the past by uncovering old objects or buildings and examining them carefully

aristocrat member of the ruling class

Australian outback dry center of Australia, where very few people live

billboard large board for advertising posters, usually found beside main roads

Buddhist someone who follows the religion of Buddhism. Buddhists believe that you should not become too attached to material things. They also believe that you live many lives in different bodies.

clan group of people who share the same ancestors and customs

classical belonging to the period of the ancient Greeks and Romans. Classical art is art in the same style as the Greeks and Romans.

composer someone who writes music

contemporary belonging to the modern world

Cubism style of art in which painters built up their pictures using a collection of geometric shapes. The Cubist movement began in the early years of the 20th century.

depression strong feeling of sadness and misery

elder oldest member of a group of people

elemental based on nature's elements, fire, air, water and earth

environment natural world all around us

estuary part of a river, where it meets the sea

formal carefully and deliberately arranged

fresco wall painting done on wet plaster

grotto a garden feature consisting of a semi-enclosed leafy area

Impressionist style of painting in which artists try to show the impression that something has on their senses

installation artwork involving sound, light, or video that is installed (set up) in a gallery

Islamic the civilization developed by Muslims, who follow the religion Islam

ladies-in-waiting women who look after an important lady, such as a queen

land art very large-scale sculptures in the landscape

landscape gardening art of designing gardens so that they look like natural landscapes

maze pattern of paths, made as a puzzle for people to find their way through

medieval belonging to the period from approximately 1000 C.E. to 1450 C.E.

meditate to think deeply and peacefully as part of a mental exercise

melodramatic very dramatic and exaggerated in style

Middle Ages period of history between approximately 1000 C.E. to 1450 C.E.

Moors Islamic people who arrived in Spain from North Africa around 700 C.E. The Moors ruled southern Spain for over 400 years.

Mughals Islamic people who arrived in India around 1500 C.E. The Mughals ruled northern India for over 300 years.

palette knife small knife with a wide blade, used for scraping paint off a palette (board used for paints). Some artists use a palette knife to apply paint thickly to their paintings.

panorama very wide view

perspective system used by artists to show things in the distance

pigment paint made from natural materials such as earth

pilgrimage journey to a holy place

primary colors red, yellow, and blue. Primary colors can be mixed to produce all the others colors.

realistic very like the real thing

Renaissance movement in art and learning that took place in Europe between the 14th and 16th centuries. Renaissance artists aimed to produce more realistic works of art than before and were partly inspired by the art of the ancient Greeks and Romans.

Rococo style of art and architecture that uses graceful lines and delicate colors. The Rococo style is playful and lighthearted. It flourished in Europe in the 18th century.

Romantic style of art and writing that concentrates on feelings and emotions. The Romantic movement began in the late 18th century and flourished in the early 19th century.

sacred holy

sculpture work of art made from stone, wood, metal, or other materials

sepia kind of brown ink used by artists

Stuarts royal family that ruled England from 1603 to 1714

tapestry heavy piece of cloth with pictures or patterns woven into it

tomb grave, usually for an important person

Tudors royal family that ruled England from 1485 to 1603

watercolor type of painting using paints that can be mixed with water

Index